THE CELEBRATED STORY

OF

HONEY WINE

THE H◯ |||||||||||||||||||||||||| Y

Published by
The Honey Wine Company LLC
San Francisco, California
U.S.A.

www.DiscoverHoneyWine.org

ISBN 978-0-9893339-0-0 Hardback
ISBN 978-0-9893339-1-7 Paperback
ISBN 978-0-9893339-2-4 Ebook

First Edition

Dedication

*To three determined groups who operate
in challenging environments:*

———————

T'ej makers and *t'ej* bar owners in Ethiopia who
continue to resist the onslaught of well financed
and promoted pilsner style commercial beers.

Organizers and participants of The Mazer Cup in the
U.S.A. who have stuck by their mead
regardless of what everyone else is drinking.

Independent farmers and beekeepers
around the world.

Pleasant words are a honeycomb,
sweet to the soul
and healing to the bones.

- Proverbs 16:24

ደስ የሚያሰኝ ቃል የማር ወለላ ነው፤
ለነፍስ ጣፋጭ፤
ለዐጥንትም ፈውስ ነው።

- ምሳሌ ፲፮፥፳፬

TABLE OF CONTENTS

FOREWORD   1
PREFACE   3
INTRODUCTION   9

CHAPTER I. AN ANCIENT LIBATION   12
THE RISE OF CULTURE   12
A LONG TIME AGO IN A FIELD FAR, FAR AWAY   13
AFRICAN ORIGINS?   14
HONEY WINE IN THE MEDITERRANEAN   17
HONEY WINE IN EUROPE   20
A GLOBAL PHENOMENON   21
THE GREAT HONEY WINE RECESSION   23

CHAPTER II. GOLDEN WINE: CHARACTER AND VARIETY   26
ACQUAINT YOURSELF WITH GREATNESS   26
LOVE AT FIRST SIGHT   27
MISUNDERSTANDING IS SUCH SWEET SORROW   28
NO TANNINS, PLEASE   30
A WINE FOR ALL SEASONS   31
MELLOWING HONEY WINE WITH FRUIT   32
THE SPICE OF LIFE   33
A GRAPE WAY TO SERVE HONEY WINE   34
FOR THE LOVE OF BEER AND HONEY WINE   36

CHAPTER III. HOW TO SERVE HONEY WINE   38
OF TEMPERATURES AND GLASSES   38
FOOD PAIRINGS   40
For Your Dry Humor   40
The Semi-Sweet Life   41
Sweets to the Sweet   43
FOR THE MIXOLOGISTS   45
Honey Wine Mimosa   45
The Kentucky Honeymoon   46
Long Island Honey Wine   46
The Honeyrita   47
Tequila Honey-Rise   47
The Honey Wine Toddy   48

CHAPTER IV. THE MOST SUSTAINABLE LIBATION   50
THE BUZZ ON BEES   51
DRINK HONEY WINE, SAVE THE FORESTS   54
A BEELINE FOR URBAN RENEWAL   56
WHY YOU SHOULD KEEP IT LOCAL   58
AN UN-INDUSTRIAL REVOLUTION   60

CHAPTER V. A BEVERAGE OF MYTHICAL PROPORTIONS   62
HONEYMOON IN BABYLON   62
HONEY LOVE   63
POETIC INSPIRATION   66

CHAPTER VI. "MUST" KNOWS ABOUT FERMENTATION   68
FLOWERS LIVE IN THE BOUQUET OF HONEY   68
HOLY YEASTIES!   70
GOOD CHEMISTRY MEANS GOOD WINE   72
FOLLOW THE YELLOW BRICK ROAD   73
GOT GESHO?   74
DO TRY THIS AT HOME   75

CHAPTER VII. THE REBIRTH OF HONEY WINE   78

ACKNOWLEDGEMENTS   82

HOW TO ORDER HONEY WINE IN ANY LAND   84

Foreword

The worst thing about history is that we have to take other people's word for it. No matter how vivid the account of something that happened decades or centuries ago, we'll never really know what it looked like, felt like, sounded like or smelled like to be there.

Nor what it tasted like. Some 2,000 years ago, a lucky Aksumite discovered *t'ej*, the wonderful Ethiopian honey wine, and he probably didn't even know what he'd just tasted. I say 2,000 years because the earliest written record of *t'ej* dates back that far. But it may well have been – in fact, almost certainly was – even longer ago.

Aksum was the great ancient kingdom that occupied the northern portion of modern Ethiopia, most of modern Eritrea, and portions of Arabia; and the Aksumites left behind enough artifacts and inscriptions for us to understand a fair bit about their habits. We know they ate lentils and peas, two items familiar from the Ethiopian dinner table, and that they used *teff*, probably to make *injera*, the Ethiopian traditional bread. We also know they drank *t'ej*.

I wish I could remember the first time I tasted *t'ej*, but alas, that moment of personal history is lost to time. I began making it myself at home eight years ago with honey from local markets and with gesho, the woody hops that flavors the *t'ej*, from Ethiopian markets in Washington, D.C. The first batch fermented well, and day by day, for five weeks, I watched my *t'ej* come to fruition.

I soon named my *t'ej* and, just for fun, created a label. You can read about Ferenj Tej at my website, *All About Tej*, or in my book, *Mesob Across America: Ethiopian Food in the U.S.A.*

But my interest has *just* been *t'ej*. Now, thanks to The Honey Wine Company, you can learn about all types of mead in The *Celebrated Story of Honey Wine*, a lively and readable little book loaded with information and colorful images. Honey wine may well be the oldest fermented drink in the world, and people certainly imbibed in it long before recorded history first documented it.

The Celebrated Story of Honey Wine is a valuable book that brings together a world of information that will delight both mead maniacs and the more general wine aficionado. Just be sure to have a glass of honey wine at your side as you read it.

Harry Kloman
University of Pittsburgh

Preface

In 1852, *Uncle Tom's Cabin* was published by Harriet Beecher Stowe, as was *Childhood* by Leo Tolstoy. The Palace of Westminster opened in Great Britain a month or so before Napoleon III ascended to the throne and the Presidency of the French Republic. The Second Burmese War was fought over eight months, while the Battle of Gur Amba occupied just the better part of one day.

You must be wondering, "why the history lesson?" This is *The Celebrated Story of Honey Wine*, not Jeopardy category, "1852."

Well, 1852 was a very special year for me, for you, and for one American priest. In addition to these global happenings, it was the year Rev. Lorenzo Lorraine Langstroth patented the modern frame beehive that would revolutionize honey production globally.

The year is 2009, and I am driving in the mountain rain forests of Kafa in southwestern Ethiopia with a South African *grape* winemaker. We had met just weeks before through a random stranger I met one night at a bar in the town of Stellenbosch, South Africa. The stranger, whose name I came to know as Amanuel, was an Eritrean student at the University. Upon hearing my interest in wine, Amanuel would tell me, and those with us, about a winemaker named Hilko Hegewisch, with whom he recently shared a hospital room.

I suppose they had lots of time exploring common interests because Amanuel knew of Hilko's affinity for *t'ej*. On the other hand, put a *Habesha* and a curious oenologist together in a room for a few seconds, not several days, and the topic of *t'ej* would not have to wait for awkward silence[1].

I would meet Hilko, along with his wife, Andrea, and their two sons, for dinner at a restaurant in downtown Stellenbosch the next day. Hilko took up my invitation and was on a plane to Ethiopia to research *t'ej* production within weeks. Shortly after his visit, Hilko began producing his version of honey wine under the Solms Delta label.

Kafa forest is the origin of the eponymous beverage, coffee. It's an internationally recognized biosphere reserve to conserve wild coffee genes, and an ecosystem under heavy threat of deforestation. This is a relatively lush part of Ethiopia, but I took particular notice of slash and burn activities on the long drive from Addis to Jimma and into the town of Bonga in Kafa.

The percent of native forest cover in Ethiopia has shrunk from 40% to the low single digits within a century. This is mainly driven by the rural population increases; from 35 million to 90 million over the last 35 years alone.

---

[1] Amanuel magically reappeared in the living room of a shared apartment in Cape Town where I stayed during New Years 2011.

What I witnessed in Kafa during those few days in 2009 was pressure to deforest, and the near universal use of pre-Langstroth traditional beehives (with no internal frame structures). The long bamboo or wood cylindrical enclosures are hung from tall trees, and typically, wild bees may inhabit five out of 10 of these enclosures and turn them into beehives.

These traditional hives yield only 15 pounds of honey each annually. The beekeepers have to crush the combs to extract the honey, so the bees will have to put their energy into producing new combs, not honey, the following year. But with a "modern" 1852 frame hive, the beekeeper extracts the honey through centripetal force and returns the original frame comb to the box hive; yields on frame hives average 75 pounds per year incredibly raising household income five fold.

With traditional hives, women in Kafa are effectively cut out of the beekeeping business, a relatively high income earning activity even with low-yielding traditional hives, because of taboos against women climbing trees. Moreover, dozens of beekeepers die or are crippled from falling from trees in the process of hanging the hives, and forest fires start from crudely smoking out bees when the embers easily reach the tree branches. Finally, the quality of the honey from traditional hives can be poor and inconsistent for a number of reasons (see the 90-second video on our website; it shows how hives are hung and how they are collected for harvest in Kafa).

A self-enforcing cycle of poverty causes the Kafa area residents to cut more trees to sell as firewood and to clear for corn, coffee and other crops. Ironically, less trees means less floral forage for bees so even less honey production results, not to mention the carbon dioxide emissions that result when carbon stored in trees is released upon burning.

This question crossed my mind and took hold of me ever since: Could it be that the lowly 1852 invention by the Rev. Langstroth could reverse multiple economic, environmental and social ills? More honey from modern frame hives results more household income and a more equitable gender distribution of that income—with the resultant benefits accruing to children.

Larger income on its own may or may not lead to less deforestation, but in this case, the beekeepers are keenly aware that the pollen for their honey comes from tree flowers, so they will surely not kill the proverbial goose that lays the golden eggs.

How to pay for these hives? Well, why not add even more value and produce honey wine (in Ethiopia) using honey bought directly from Kafa beekeepers and export it globally? The plan was to use some of the honey wine proceeds to fund the conversion of thousands of traditional hives to modern ones.

The decision of *where* and *how* to produce this wine evolved and the rest of the story spans five years, covers three countries, and could have produced a separate book.

I decided to produce our wine in Northern California for both personal and business reasons; it is where I grew up and have family, the wine industry infrastructure is strong, good quality honey is locally available and California is a very large wine market.

As luck, or destiny, would have it, I reconnected with colleagues at Wildlife Works; a pioneering California based company that works on "Reducing Emissions from Deforestation and Degradation" or REDD, and today we are attempting to develop a REDD project in Kafa with modern hives as a key livelihood alternative to cutting trees for crop agriculture. The project would create jobs and share carbon credit revenues with Kafa communities and with the local government.

The Honey Wine Company will initially use all local honey, buying directly from California beekeepers and farmers. But the original plan of funding modern beehive conversions in Kafa still remains. Our long-term plan is to source some specialty Kafa honey produced in modern hives for ultra-exclusive lines of wine.

Many issues were resolved by locating production in the U.S.A. But all is not well with California beekeepers because of a very serious problem called beehive Colony Collapse Disorder (CCD), which is characterized by bees abandoning their hives, leading to decreased crop pollination, a reduction in honey output and commensurate increase in price. There are efforts aimed at finding a solution to CCD, and The Honey Wine Company intends to support initiatives, such as California based Project Apis m., by creating awareness and donating funds from the sale of wine.

I have shared how the wine came to be, but nothing about the book. We wrote it because a vast majority of people have never heard of, much less tasted, honey wine. So I wanted you to know about its history, how it tastes and pairs with food, how it is made and what the environmental issues are.

I hope that *The Celebrated Story of Honey Wine* will help you savor the history and culture of this ancient drink as well as its unforgettable taste.

Ayele Solomon
The Honey Wine Company
San Francisco, September 2013

For the FREE ebook and podcast, visit DiscoverHoneyWine.org

Don't just read about it, taste it! Of course my favorite is Bee d'Vine. TASTE CHANGE at beedvine.com

Introduction

When Harry Potter first tried honey wine, he enjoyed it immensely, but he also remarked that he had never had anything like it before. Like Harry, so many of us have been immediately captivated by our first taste of

what the ancients called "the nectar of the gods." But even though golden-toned honey wine was a favorite long before the Queen of Sheba was tipping royal cups of it around 950 B.C., many of us have yet to have the unique privilege of tasting honey wine for the first time.

Because of this, honey wine (historically known as "mead" in English, and "hydromel" or honey water, in French) is largely misunderstood. And that's why we've written a story to awaken and celebrate the rich past and resplendent character of the noblest beverage on earth. Our story will explore how honey wine has influenced history and myth on its way from ancient civilization to your table.

Best of all, our story has a happy ending. Because today we are triumphantly calling an end to "The Great Honey Wine Recession." It's been a long time coming, but honey wine is back to enliven and illuminate the way modern imbibers eat, drink, and enjoy special moments.

So while you're free to drink it as the Vikings did (with epic gusto, no doubt), we intend to show you how sun-kissed honey wine is the modern, sustainable alternative to beer and grape wine. The oldest libation in history will taste refreshingly new as you pair it with your food, friends, and special occasions. But even more refreshing is the role honey wine will play in helping to save our critically threatened bee populations. In a time in which we've seen the rebirth of farmers markets and local, sustainable foods, the environmentally responsible craft of making honey wine makes more sense than ever.

For those in the know, no libation enchants quite like honey wine. That's because thousands of years of practice have made it perfectly suited to your divinely inspired moments. We know that you'll enjoy the rich story of honey wine as you get to know the oldest new beverage on the market. And as you read, you'll become part of the greatest comeback story in drinking history. So what will you add to the tale?

To your health!

Chapter I. An Ancient Libation

The Rise of Culture

Honey wine practically *is* history. Claude Lévi-Strauss, the renowned French anthropologist, wrote that the invention of honey wine marked the point at which  humans moved "from nature to culture." This is a big deal. Not just any drink could inspire humankind's first foray into cultured living. To pull this feat off, a drink would have to be around for a very, very long time. But even more crucially, it would have to contain the power to elevate us from our natural state. Honey wine certainly has the pedigree and character to answer both of these calls.

So what were the prime ingredients that sparked human culture? Well, the ingredients are as simply wonderful as the final product. All humans needed to kick start culture were bees, flowers, sunshine, water, and naturally occurring yeasts. Every monumental achievement in human history has its competing stories, so let's take a closer look at how honey wine brought all of us a bit closer to the gods.

A Long Time Ago in a Field Far, Far Away

About 150 million years ago, flowers began popping up on earth. And then about 10 to 20 million years ago, bees became social insects that specialized in gathering nectar and pollinating flowers. Of course, there were no humans around at the time, but bees were already busily making honey for their own purposes.

Bees had plenty of time to perfect honey production before humans popped on the scene about 200,000 years ago. While humans were still trying to figure out that bees make delicious sweetness, the busy socialites of the insect world had long before figured out that water was no good for their honey. Well, at least not for them, because water makes honey ferment (and thus intoxicating). Bees had their own clever methods for keeping the honeycomb watertight, but the good news is that happy accidents happen. And when happy accidents happen between bees, flowers, water, and sunshine, humans win! These are the prime elements that make honey wine the most sustainable alcoholic beverage the world has ever known. For more on that story, check out Chapter Four on bees and sustainability.

African Origins?

Many locate Africa as the origin of the happy accident that is honey wine. Picture the scene: wild bees doing their thing in a seasonal climate that features dramatically arid and rainy seasons. These bi-polar weather patterns caused hollows to form in baobab and miombo trees where elephants had ripped off branches. Bees would then build hives in these hollows during the dry season. And when the wet season came, these nooks would often fill with water. As soon as honey, water, sunshine, and some native yeast get together, honey wine is a natural result.

Imagine the lucky hunter-gatherer that discovered honey wine while looking for a snack. In this scenario, it's easy to see why honey wine has been called a "gift from the gods." But it's equally plausible that a hunter on a long trip partially emptied his water vessel to store some newly found honey. After the long trip home, conditions might have been just right for spontaneous fermentation, which of course would have made our happy traveler a hometown hero—if not a god.

The rich and royal history of honey wine in Ethiopia makes it natural to think of Africa as the birthplace of the ancient beverage. The Ethiopian word for honey wine is "*t'ej*" [t'ədʒ], an Amharic word [ጠጅ] long used to signify a drink intimately woven into the history and culture of Ethiopia. One of the ways *t'ej* is unique among honey wines is the use of gesho to make it (see our "Got Gesho?" chapter for more on that). Ethiopian's love *t'ej* so much they eventually made it their national drink. And why not? After all, Ethiopians pour more honey wine today than they do beer and grape wine, and probably more honey wine than all of the countries in the world put together! Visit Harry Kloman's legendary *t'ej* website today and become a *t'ej* scholar overnight.

The story about how *t'ej* became the Ethiopian drink of choice begins about a thousand years before the birth of Christ. Legend tells us that the Queen of Sheba lavished opulent gifts on King Solomon during a diplomatic voyage. Among the gold, precious stones, and exotic spices was some royal quality *t'ej*. And it's worth noting that this *t'ej* might have played an inspirational role in Sheba's greatest gift to Solomon: a baby boy named Menelik who later become king of Ethiopia. Tradition holds that Menelik brought the Ark of the Covenant to Ethiopia after visiting his father in Jerusalem, so he was indeed a very important baby.

Centuries later, in 1270 A.D., the Ethiopian monarch, Yekuno Amlak, evoked the legend of Sheba and Solomon while declaring himself the direct descendant of Menelik. This brilliant political move ushered in the Solomonic dynasty of Ethiopian emperors that went on to rule the nation until 1974. Even to this day, t'ej remains the everyday drink of the people, while premium varieties of the libation are reserved to bless weddings. Even Muslims who abstain from alcohol will commonly drink the non-alcoholic variety of t'ej, or berz as it is called.

It just goes to show that one never knows what might happen when sharing honey wine as a gift. The magnanimous gesture of gifting honey wine might reshape an entire nation's history, politics, and culture. Or (on a slightly smaller scale) the gift might make you a friend for life.

Whatever the case, when you enjoy t'ej be sure to celebrate the occasion by raising your berillé (a round-bottom glass flask used exclusively for t'ej) or your horn carved wancha with a rousing "Letenachin". That's the Amharic word for "to our health".

Honey Wine in the Mediterranean

In the legendary "Golden Age," the Greeks were said to have lived in a paradise setting replete with everything needed for the ideal life, including abundantly delicious food and drink. Could it be that honey wine put the "Gold" in the Golden Age?

Given the way that ancient Greek and Roman authors write about honey wine, it's easy to suspect that it was the drink of choice when gods and humans lived, played, and loved together. Aristotle (384 B.C.) writes copiously about honey wine in *Meteorologica*, and the Roman philosopher, Pliny the Elder (22 B.C.), puts his early connoisseurship for the libation on display in his book *Naturalis Historia*. Columella (a Roman naturalist) even gives a good recipe for making honey wine in his book *De re Rustica* around 60 A.D.:

Take rainwater kept for several years, and mix a sextarius of this water with a pound of honey. For a weaker mead, mix a sextarius of water with nine ounces of honey. The whole is exposed to the sun for 40 days, and then left on a shelf near the fire. If you have no rainwater, then boil spring water.

If you try this formula, you might decide against storing rainwater for several years, but you had better measure out your sextari with precision—whatever those might be. For more on how honey wine is fermented today, take a look at "Good Chemistry Means Good Wine" in Chapter Six.

Greek and Roman legend both identify honey wine as ambrosia, or the "Food of the Gods." So yeah, these people liked their honey wine. The ancient Roman poet Ovid (43 B.C.) writes that Bacchus gave humans honey wine as a gift, and it's true that before Bacchus was called the "God of Wine" he was known as "The Honey-Lord." In fact, he even carried a *thyrsus* (or staff) that was dripping with honey. The honey-laden *thyrsus* was

a powerfully suggestive symbol of sexual potency and fertility. If you're into suggestive associations, you can read more about the aphrodisiac qualities of honey wine in our "Honey Love" story found in Chapter Five covering mythology.

Just as in Africa, honey wine was central in both the myths and everyday life of ancient Greeks and Romans.

And this was especially true of the *metheglin* variety, or "The Spice of Life", covered in Chapter Two, which was thought to be the highest form of superior taste and culture. According to Ken Schramm, author of *The Compleat Meadmaker*, "The gods and the wealthy sipped" on honey wine and the literature of ancient Greece habitually used "honey and sweetness as superlative descriptions of wines." Simply put, honey wine was a mark of class and distinction that rose to the heights of Mount Olympus.

Schramm also notes that ancient Greek and Roman tastes for honey wine have been tragically overshadowed by later Italian tastes for grape wine. Grape wine has dominated the modern market for so long that we have begun to lose our perspective. But no more! A new Golden Age of honey wine is upon us.

Honey Wine in Europe

By now there are a host of Eurocentrics shouting at the top of their lungs about Europe's preeminence in honey wine. And along with their voices, there is an abundance of proof that honey wine has a long, rich history spanning from pre-Roman Europe through the Renaissance.

Strangely enough, strong evidence of honey wine in Europe pops up around the same time as stories about the Queen of Sheba of the Axum Empire and King Solomon in Israel. For example, cauldrons with ancient honey wine residue that dates back to 1000 B.C. have been discovered in Germany and the British Isles. As if ancient cauldrons weren't cool enough, there was honey wine in them.

Recent evidence has even been gathered that strongly suggests that very early Europeans were fermenting alcohol in the Bronze Age (3600-600 B.C.). Given the naturally simple way that honey ferments when removed from the hive, it's more than reasonable to conclude that honey wine was among the earliest (if not the first) alcoholic beverage in Europe.

Nowhere is honey wine's high cultural status among the elite more evident than in *Beowulf* (c. 700s), which retells the epic confrontation between the heroic Beowulf and the cave dwelling monster Grendel. Honey wine is clearly the only drink for kings and their greatest warriors in *Beowulf*. In fact, the epic is drenched with overflowing cups of the ceremonious libation. If *Beowulf* is the story of civilization overcoming humankind's wilder side, then honey wine is the leading symbol for civilized living in the ancient world.

Honey continued to maintain its high cultural status in Europe until the Renaissance. Because honey was initially so expensive, it was only an option for royalty and the very rich. Fortunately for us, advances in modern beekeeping have made honey wine a more economically approachable option, while still maintaining the richly inherent value of a drink deeply saturated in tradition and history.

A Global Phenomenon

While we have been focusing on a few hotspots in the ancient world, it's important to know that honey wine is a global phenomenon. The real magic of honey wine is in the way it organically emerges across diverse cultures without much evidence of cross-pollination, to borrow a phrase from the bees. Almost every language has a word for honey wine, these can be found in the "How to Order Honey Wine in Any Land" glossary. And who doesn't need more words for honey wine?

Along with all of this linguistic evidence, there's plenty of physical evidence to assert the ancient prominence of honey wine. For example, the oldest archaeological evidence to date was unearthed in northern China, where researchers discovered vessels containing a fermented mixture of honey, rice, and fruit dated to around 7000 B.C.

Maybe the Chinese were fermenting honey 6,000 years before the Africans and Europeans, or maybe we've yet to unearth even earlier evidence of honey wine in other places. Think about it. Who in the world would intentionally leave delicious honey wine lying around for thousands of years?

Whatever the case, here's the big point: given the simple, natural way that honey ferments and a seemingly universal appreciation for honey wine, we could plausibly push the date for fermentation back thousands and thousands of years. Some researchers speculate that an early knowledge of fermentation could have been lost and rediscovered again and again throughout the course of history. If honey wine really is a gift from the gods, then it makes sense that this gift would be lovingly spread to every corner of the earth.

Thankfully, we'll never lose the ability to tap into the libatious powers of honey ever again. In the meantime, we must do our best to protect our divine bee messengers—after all, they are the angels that deliver the "Nectar of the Gods."

The Great Honey Wine Recession

Honey wine is still widely popular in Ethiopia, while in other places such as Canada, Germany, New Zealand, Poland and the U.S.A., it has become a cherished secret of the discriminating few. So why did the global phenomenon that is honey wine ever recede from favor? We could devote an entire book to this question alone, but the historic price of honey is central to most theories.

One theory is that there was a drastic rise in honey prices throughout the 14th and 17th centuries. When Europeans returned home after exploring "New Worlds," many of them came back with cheap sugar cane, which could have rapidly pushed honey into a niche market. Around 1300 A.D., for example, Marco Polo returned from the Spice Islands with some of this cheap sugar cane. Honey had always been the privilege of the elite, but when the prices became prohibitive, other fermented beverages might have found new favor.

The rise in honey prices also coincided with improvements in the quality of French and Italian wines. These wines would have been a new diversion for elite alcohol enthusiasts at the same time that technological advances in brewing made beer a more stable and movable commodity for the working classes to cheaply enjoy. With high-end consumers turning more and more to grape wine and the proletariat drinking beer, the traditional luxury of honey wine receded into the world of artisanal craftsmanship—where it remains today, for the most part.

And finally, technology seems to have played a role in pushing honey wine into the category of rare pleasures. Honey wine production took a precipitous fall during the industrial revolution. After the modern frame beehive and the first centrifugal honey extractor were invented in the mid-1800s, the old way of producing honey all but died out in the western world. Prior to frame hives and centrifugal extraction, honeycombs were crushed whole and the honey was separated from the comb by pressing. In order to get all of the honey out, the honeycombs were rinsed with warm water.

Candle makers (many of whom were monks) used beeswax in their craft, and then used the honey-water byproduct to make honey wine. After the process was mechanized, there was no leftover honey-water—thus, a steep decline in the production of honey wine.

Whatever happened in the past, we can now proclaim an end to The Great Honey Wine Recession. So call your neighbors and friends and invite them to become a part of this storybook revival. The libation is returning with vigor because while mere products can come and go, artisanal crafts never die.

And now *you* can play a role in the rebirth of honey wine. Not only will you be indulging in an age-old pleasure, but your demand for high quality honey products will also help to sustain bee colonies that are facing new threats in a modern world.

For more on the bees, visit "The Buzz on Bees" in Chapter Four covering sustainability.

Chapter II. Golden Wine: Character and Variety

Acquaint Yourself with Greatness

To be great is to be misunderstood.

–Ralph Waldo Emerson

History has already established the greatness of honey wine. But greatness is often misunderstood. When Galileo proved that the earth revolves around the sun (and not vice versa) he was imprisoned and labeled a heretic. Nothing this dramatic ever happened to honey wine, but by following the path of non-conformity the most noble beverage in history has suffered from great misunderstanding.

To do away with misunderstanding, let's take a few revolutions around the golden luminescence of honey wine. Because while a honey wine centered universe may not hold up to scientific scrutiny, the idea alone is inspirational. And hey. The more you know about honey wine, the more you will enjoy it.

Love at First Sight

To look at honey wine is to fall immediately in love. Like all wines, honey wine varies in color and body, which creates a diverse field of pleasures for the connoisseur to indulgently wander. But it's the richly golden tones and gemlike clarity of a superior glass of honey wine  that immediately captures the attention of the newcomer. The golden hue of honey wine reflects the wealth and royal taste of kings and queens who favored the libation for thousands of years. And who wouldn't want to see themselves in their favorite drink?

You, on the other hand, will most likely appreciate how light fancifully dances around your glass on a summer's day, or how golden honey wine subtly provides the most illuminating accessory to your evening wear. And all of this happens before your first sip.

But before you take that first sip (or if you can't wait, just after), go ahead and swirl your honey wine around to appreciate the fullness and body of your libation as swirling gives way to legs that gently coat and caress the sides of your glass. And as you continue to gaze, one thing will become brilliantly clear: no wine looks as divine as honey wine.

Misunderstanding Is Such Sweet Sorrow

To imagine all honey wine tasting sweet is a perfectly understandable misconception. Because nothing is sweeter than honey. But think about this: grapes on the vine are about as sweet as it gets. And yet, most grape wines are not sweet. Of course they *can* be sweet - consider Ports and Rieslings, and all manner of dessert wines that cater to the sweeter side of life. All of this begs the question: how does sweet become neat and dry?

The magic transformation depends on residual sugar content, which is just a fancy way of saying how much sugar remains in wine after fermentation. During

fermentation sugar is converted to alcohol by yeast, but if the process is stopped before all of the sugar is converted to alcohol, this residual sugar hangs around to contribute to the sweetness of your wine. By varying fermentation time, honey wine artisans can happily cater to the taste sensibilities of a wide range of imbibers.

This means that the same diversity offered by grape wine is also found in the world of honey wine. Honey wines typically come in three basic categories that inform consumers where a beverage lies on the scale from dry to sweet. So while choosing a bottle, look for labels that let you know if your honey wine is dry, semi-sweet or sweet.

If you like a dry, refined beverage, honey wine has options for you. Or maybe you're all about sweetness; or maybe your taste is moody, making you like dry now and sweet later; or maybe you're somewhere in between. Okay, you're probably getting the point, which is that honey wine is as wonderfully various as grape wine.

No Tannins, Please

You know that dry, puckery sensation you get in your mouth after tasting some wines? Well, that mouth-drying bitterness comes from chemical substances called tannins that occur naturally in grape skins, stems, and seeds. Next time you're eating grapes, try tasting just the skin of a single grape—you're mouth will immediately dry out as a bitter taste transforms your palate. This is because tannins are an astringent, bitter plant compound that actually causes increased friction in your mouth, giving you a palpable sense of dryness as you smack your tongue on the roof of your palate. Yeah, you know the feeling we're talking about. While many wine drinkers enjoy the "mouthfeel" that tannins create in some grape wines, there is a significant portion of the population that simply cannot tolerate the reaction.

For these people, honey wine provides a welcome opportunity to drink tannin free wine. And the option of honey wine is especially exciting for those of us who experience "red wine headache," a commonly reported phenomenon that many experts link to high tannin levels in red wines. So if you don't want to hear, "not tonight, honey, I have a headache," consider making your honey happy with honey wine.

A Wine for All Seasons

Variety truly is the spice of life. And honey wine indulges us with a wide variety of styles. There are enthusiasts who insist that "traditional" honey wine may only consist of honey, water, and yeast. But having said this, honey wines have been quite varied over the ages, making it hard to designate one variety as traditional.

Today you can find honey wines ranging from dry to sweet and flat to bubbly. And you'll also discover adjuncts that help suit honey wine to every palate. There are traditional adjuncts like hops, herbs, spices, and fruits, but there's also some quirky wizardry going on that allows you to explore cutting edge flavors like bacon (yes, bacon!) and jalapeño. The possibilities are limitless. But before you try and wrap your head around bacon honey wine, let's first try to master the major varieties you're sure to encounter (or even make).

Mellowing Honey Wine with Fruit

Honey wines that are fermented or flavored with fruit have traditionally been called *melomels*. Any fruit can be used to enhance the taste of traditional honey wine, but some common favorites include: apples, pears, peaches, cherries, raspberries, strawberries, blueberries, and the list goes on and on. In fact, the only limit to what can be added to a *melomel* is your imagination. Grapes are also a popular addition, but since introducing grapes to honey wine results in a variety unto its own, we've reserved a section entirely devoted to varieties that incorporate grapes (check below for our section on *pyments*).

For the ancients, adding fruit to honey wine was a clever way of preserving fruit that could be enjoyed outside of its natural season. But *melomels* still represent a popular choice for home honey wine enthusiasts and typically more *melomels* are entered into honey wine competitions than other categories. Popularity cannot be denied!

The Spice of Life

While the word "*metheglin*" may sound a bit medicinal, the word really represents a truly wonderful variety that makes use of spices and herbs for fermenting or flavoring honey wine. By adding ingredients like clove, cinnamon, ginger, nutmeg, marjoram, lavender, chamomile, and/or juniper, honey wines can develop complex distinctions to suit the individual whims of their creator.

The ancient Greeks were especially fond of herb-infused wines because they were considered a mark of high culture and prestige. To understand why this would be so, we must consider the high cost of spices in a time when trade routes stretched for thousands of miles across harsh terrains and tempestuous shipping routes. Without automobiles and modern ships, spices were costly luxury items reserved for the very wealthy. Add the cost of spices to the already kingly price for honey and the phrase "golden wine" takes on new meaning.

While *metheglins* still provide richly warm aromatic notes that make them a perfect libation for parties, picnics, or to crown your holiday season, you can manage a bottle without breaking into your royal coffers.

A Grape Way To Serve Honey Wine

He syngeth, brokkynge as a nyghtyngale;
He sente hire pyment, meeth, and spided ale.
–Geoffrey Chaucer

In the 1380s, Geoffrey Chaucer was already writing about *pyments* as love gifts. And while Chaucer's English hardly resembles the language we know today, *pyment* remains a wonderfully romantic honey wine suitable for gifts of love.

Pyments are honey wines fermented with grapes, making the range of taste diversity never ending. The sheer variety of grapes alone makes *pyment* an expansive category. But the diversity multiplies when you consider that intermingling grapes and honey enables a full range of honey wines—from honey wines with subtle grape highlights to grape wines with nuanced touches of honey, there's a balance for everyone.

Whatever the balance, fermenting honey with grapes brings the best attributes of honey and grape wines pleasantly together. For those of us on the fence, *pyments* are a glorious gateway drink toward achieving the highest pleasures honey wine has to offer.

For the Love of Beer and Honey Wine

If a *pyment* is a marriage between honey and grape wines, a *braggot* is the blessed union that occurs when beer and honey wine tie the knot. But like all marriages, nothing is as simple as it seems.

The term *"braggot"* describes honey wines that make use of malted barley, hops and/ or grains. The word itself is of welsh origin, and there are references to the hybrid beverage in Ireland dating as far back as the 12th century. The intriguing combination of beer and honey wine produces a strong drink with uncommon flavors. The strength of the concoction, however, is balanced by the sweetness of the honey, which at the end of the day produces a hearty elixir that will warm the coldest winter nights.

Vikings were accustomed to simply mixing honey wine and beer crudely together after plundering a village, but since most of us have given up pillaging, we have more free time to combine honey and malts together before fermentation, which produces a much more refined drink.

Chapter III. How To Serve Honey Wine

At last Gandalf pushed away his plate and jug—he had eaten two whole loaves (with masses of butter and honey and clotted cream) and drunk at least a quart of mead—and he took out his pipe. –From: *The Hobbit* by J.R.R. Tolkien

Honey wine is a remarkably versatile drink that compliments and even enhances a host of variously delicious foods.

When it comes to serving temperature and food pairings, you must first consider what variety you're using to enhance your favorite food, friends, and occasions. For a refresher on the different varieties of honey wine, refer back to Chapter Two.

Of Temperatures and Glasses

For honey wines on the drier side of the spectrum, anywhere from cellar temperature to chilled is generally preferred. Serving dry honey wine at cooler temperatures enhances the bouquet and allows the delicate complexities of the wine to be discerned before the dry finish. For sweeter honey wines, serving at room temperature enables the sweetness, aroma, and rich, flavor to fully come through. And for the holiday season, warm honey wine mulled with spices is always a welcome way to chase the cold away after a long day of shopping. And when you mull honey wine, the aroma of holiday cheer will entirely envelop your home.

As for glassware, either an oversized wine glass or snifter provides a marvelous vessel to display and enjoy your honey wine. But if the moment calls for classic elegance, a small flute presents grace and sophistication. And we strongly recommend serving honey wine in a clear glass presented on a table covered with a white tablecloth—this will allow the brilliant, golden hues of honey wine to fully shine upon your occasion. Finally, a hearty mug or chalice will serve well to evoke the days of old as you sip warm goodness on a cold, cold night.

Still, when it comes to moments of pleasure, you should always follow your own way rather than follow the traditional advice of "experts." When it comes to honey wine, you're the expert—go ahead and experiment.

Food Pairings

It simply is not enough to ask what food goes well with honey wine. Because *first*, you need to consider which variety of honey wine you're serving. Just as with grape wine or beer, the variety determines the food pairing. So without further ado:

For Your Dry Humor

Similar to white grape wines (like Pinot Grigio or Sauvignon Blanc), the dry variety of honey wines are wonderful any time of year, but especially refreshing during the warm months of summer. In this spirit, dry honey wines pair well with most seafood, including: shellfish, sushi, and grilled fish. If you're pairing a dry fruit-based honey wine, try drawing out the fruit with sushi—maybe a wasabi raw tuna salad would do best. But you also can't lose while pairing your dry honey wine with Cajun shrimp or oysters, because spicy food is a good companion with almost all honey varieties. A classic grilled halibut with a basil pesto topping would also companion nicely with a good bottle of dry honey wine.

But you're certainly not limited to seafood. Dry varieties are wonderful with rich, creamy starters and dips—if you're serving spinach or artichoke dip with French bread, serve a dry honey wine to kick-start your guests' appetite for the rest of your meal. And if the rest of that meal includes dishes like Chicken Florentine or spinach stuffed pablano peppers, you might as well keep serving that honey wine all night. And don't forget creamy pasta dishes such as Fettuccine Alfredo while pairing with dry varieties. You can also bring the honey theme

to the fore by serving the dry variety alongside honey-baked ham studded with cloves and coated with a tangy glaze.

As for dessert, keep it light with the dry variety. A simple plate of strawberries, melons or pineapples would always go well with dry honey wine. Enjoy!

The Semi-Sweet Life

A brisk swirl of your semi-sweet glass of honey wine will release a pleasantly sweet nose that will compliment almost any elegantly simple cheese and fruit plate starter—or, since we're talking starters, try a semi-sweet with some roasted garlic spread on your favorite crusty bread or crackers. Amazing.

After starters, the slightly lighter taste of the semi-sweet variety will pair well with pork, chicken, and pheasant dishes. And if you're looking to kick it up a notch, the synergy that happens when semi-sweets pair with barbecue and spiced foods is utterly incomparable. Spicy Thai entrees go especially well with a semi-sweet, as will spiced Mexican, Indian, and Ethiopian cuisines. Especially Ethiopian food. Do yourself a favor and find your local Ethiopian restaurant. When you do, consider a semi-sweet with *shiro*, a traditional chickpea dish that absolutely demands honey wine. Honey wine is deeply imbedded in Ethiopian culture, and when you taste the food with the wine, you'll forever be hooked.

Korean barbecue chicken also comes to mind when thinking about optimal pairings. In fact, barbecue of any kind will find a mutual companion in a semi-sweet. And finally, curry, curry, curry. Spicy veggie curries or

curried chicken are top-notch fits for semis. If you're having Indian or Indonesian cuisine, you'd be well advised to take the semi route.

The semi-sweet variety pairs awesomely with almost any dessert, but you absolutely must indulge in a chocolate cake pairing. No really, you must.

Sweets to the Sweet

And now to our just desserts. Ah, but you'll have to wait...for a moment at least. Because sweet honey wines are not just for dessert. For example, the sweet

variety pairs extraordinarily well with strong tasting cheeses. Blue cheeses, for example, have a strong taste that can overpower a timid wine. Because blue cheeses are relatively salty, they tend to find better compliments in sweeter wines, making the sweet variety an obvious choice for blues. And because sweet honey wines with a good acid backbone naturally cleanse the palate, they make the taste of each new bite as intense as the first. The same can be said for most aged cheeses, so be sure to experiment to find some heavenly combinations.

Sweet honey wines also go well with entrees that stand up to sweetness, such as again, the spiced foods from Africa, Asia and India. And a warm, hearty stew always goes well with a sweet honey wine.

Okay, back to desserts (yay!). Sweet honey wines are *the* libation for closing out the night: they pair perfectly with dessert pastries, rich chocolate dishes, and any creamy dessert (preferably with buttery caramel sauce all over it). Try chocolate mousse cake. Or apple pie with ginger. And sweet honey wine goes great with nut-based desserts. In the end, sweet wines work with almost any dessert, so long as the balance of sweetness and acidity can carry the sugars off without cloying the palate.

Finally, don't forget that sweet honey wines are a dessert unto themselves. So put a crown on any meal with a golden glass of honey wine.

Bon appétit.

For the Mixologists

If you frequent popular nightspots, you know that mixology is all the rage right now. And honey wine is definitely in the mix when it comes to creative cocktails that add to the character of your occasion. But you don't have to go out to enjoy mixology. Why not stay in and entertain your friends with drinks they never imagined existed. Whatever your taste for cocktails, honey wine can make an old favorite a dazzling new experience. Here are some recipes to get you started:

Honey Wine Mimosa

Thinking Sunday brunch with friends? Don't settle for the same old mimosa. Instead, go with a Honey Wine Mimosa. It's so easy to make. Just mix 2 parts sparkling Honey Wine with 1 part orange juice, and enjoy.

❖ 2 parts sparkling honey wine
❖ 1 part orange juice

The Kentucky Honeymoon

Or maybe you're having friends over for the Kentucky Derby. This of course calls for some Kentucky bourbon...and honey wine. We call this The Kentucky Honeymoon. You mix 2 parts dry honey wine with one part bourbon, and serve it on the rocks with a sprig of fresh mint as garnish:

- ❖ 2 parts dry honey wine
- ❖ 1 part bourbon

Long Island Honey Wine

And for those warm summer evenings on the porch, you can't go wrong with honey wine's answer to the Long Island Iced Tea:

- ❖ ½ oz each of gin, vodka, rum, and triple sec
- ❖ Four shots of honey wine (either traditional or *melomel*)
- ❖ Serve on ice in a tall glass with a splash of Coke & lime wedge

The Honeyrita

If tequila is your thing, honey wine has a way of transforming old favorites into fresh alternatives. Check out both of these south of the border surprises. First, The Honeyrita. Into a shaker, pour 1 ounce tequila, ½ ounce Grand Marnier, 2 ounces of traditional honey wine, 1 ounce of non-pulp orange juice, and 1 teaspoon of fresh honey. Add a tiny pinch of sea salt and ice, and shake well. Pour into a glass rimmed with sugar. Mmm...so refreshing!

- ❖ 1 ounce tequila
- ❖ 1/2 ounce Grand Marnier
- ❖ 2 ounces of traditional honey wine
- ❖ 1 ounce orange juice (strained)
- ❖ ½ ounce fresh squeezed lime juice (strained)
- ❖ 1 teaspoon fresh honey

Tequila Honey-Rise

Next, try a delicious Tequila Honey-Rise. Mix one ounce of tequila, ½ ounce Grand Marnier or Cointreau, and a splash of orange juice in a shaker of honey wine. Serve over ice and garnish with a wedge of lime.

- ❖ 1 ounce tequila
- ❖ ½ ounce Grand Marnier or Cointreau
- ❖ A splash of orange juice
- ❖ A shaker of honey wine

The Honey Wine Toddy

And finally, honey wine offers the warm and cozy with some wonderful hot toddy alternatives, such as The Honey Wine Toddy. You mix 1 ½ ounces of your favorite whiskey with 2 ounces of heated traditional or *metheglin* honey wine, ¼ ounce of fresh honey and ¼ ounce of lemon juice. Serve this soothing mixture in a warm mug, sprinkle some cinnamon on top, and garnish it with a cinnamon stick. Put your feet up, sip, and ahhhhh.

- ❖ 1½ ounces of your favorite whiskey
- ❖ 2 ounces heated traditional or *metheglin* honey wine
- ❖ ¼ tablespoon of fresh honey
- ❖ ¼ ounce lemon juice

These few recipes are just the start. The real fun is practicing your own mixology. And because honey wine is versatile, adaptable, and delicious, you're well on your way to crafting your own signature drinks. Be sure to share. Cheers!

Chapter IV. The Most Sustainable Libation

If the bees disappeared off the surface of the globe, then man would only have four years of life left.

–Albert Einstein

Did you know that one-third of the U.S. food supply depends on pollination from bees? Without bees, so many varieties of fruits, vegetables, and even nuts would be threatened with extinction. And over the past fifteen years, 90% of the wild bee population has died out from a convergence of environmental threats.

The lifeblood of future agricultural sustainability is our bees. And the recent devastation of wild bees means that we will depend on local beekeepers to stand as the last line of defense for the well being of bees *and* the foods you love. The good news is that the more honey wine you drink, the more local beekeepers are empowered to care for the health of their hives. By helping to take honey wine into the mainstream market, you are actively contributing to the healthy balance of a planet that desperately needs bees to help sustain a rapidly growing population.

So go ahead and indulge in honey wine—after all, no other libation plays such a vital role in sustaining the planet. Honey wine producers are deeply invested in raising awareness around the plight of bees, and what better way to raise awareness than talking with your friends about the importance of bees while enjoying a glass of honey wine?

The Buzz on Bees

Helping to save the bees is just one factor that makes honey wine the most sustainable alcoholic beverage on Earth. Keep reading to find out more— and let's keep that "buzz" going.

Bees and flowers have thrived together for millions and millions of years. Their harmonious symbiotic existence gives us our most delicious and nutritious foods, with honey wine serving as the literal embodiment of the ancient love affair between bees and flowers.

And the relationship between bees and flowers is beautifully simple: flowers produce nectar to attract bees; bees gather nectar to make honey; and, in the process, bees spread the pollen needed to produce one-third of everything you eat (and drink).

But over the last two decades, environmental factors have contributed to what scientists call "Colony Collapse

Disorder" (CCD). CCD has decimated bee populations around the world. And to make matters worse, there is no single cause for CCD. While scientists are still grappling with the causes, three interconnected factors are clearly implicated: shrinking natural environments, pesticides, and invasive mites.

As natural environments shrink in favor of human development, flower populations dramatically decrease. As a result, there are not enough flowers secreting pollen and nectar to sustain hives, which leads to bee malnutrition and disease. Moreover, the flowers the bees can find are often tainted with pesticides that harm hives.

For example, researchers have recently reported a direct link between CCD and imidacloprid, a widely used pesticide that disrupts the central nervous systems of insects. Imidacloprid remains toxic throughout entire growing seasons, meaning that bees are exposed to the pesticide while gathering nectar during flowering times. Researchers also believe that imidacloprid makes bees vulnerable to parasites, which might explain why recent invasions of tracheal and varroa mites have been so deadly. This is one very important reason to consider purchasing organic products. Our pollinators deserve better.

While all of this might sound dreadfully apocalyptic, each and every remaining hive is good news for a sustainable future. Which of course makes local beekeepers a global treasure. While 90% of wild bees have died out, beekeepers have had much better success at protecting cultivated hives. If it were not for dedicated beekeepers and invested entomologists stewarding beehives, we might already be experiencing food shortages.

As we move forward, cultivated hives might entirely sustain our agricultural well-being. Grape wine and beer have dominated the alcoholic beverage category for a long time, but even a subtle shift in purchasing trends that favored honey wine would greatly incentivize local, artisanal beekeepers to produce the quantity and variety of honey needed to supply a growing industry. By keeping honey in high demand, you also help to insure the future of our greatest allies in food production. And the bees will thank you with bountiful contributions to your food and drink.

With all of this in mind, let's all raise a glass of divine honey wine in support of life-giving bees. Doesn't it feel good to give new meaning to the phrase "drink responsibly?" Cheers!

Drink Honey Wine, Save the Forests

Aside from the high ecological value bees provide as pollinators, we should also be aware of how modern beekeeping can help prevent deforestation in some of our most precious ecosystems. In China, for example, the World Wildlife Fund (WWF) is working to modernize beekeeping methods as part of a plan to save panda habitats. The WWF knows that profitable alternatives to logging mean more trees and happy pandas.

And while logging provides profits for international corporations, honey flows smoothly into nearby farmers markets, stimulating the local economy in a balanced and sustainable way. Similar efforts are underway in Ethiopia, where more honey production means less destruction of tropical rainforests. Bees produce the most honey when their environment is closest to its natural state. So in a world where profit often determines environmental impact, profitable beekeeping creates incentives for local businesses to maintain pristine forests for bees to do their magic.

Ethiopia is also working to upgrade from traditional to modern beehives. By upgrading to modern beehives, Ethiopian beekeepers are able to harvest honey without destroying the entire honeycomb. By removing honey supers without disturbing the continuity of the hive and its natural cycles, beekeepers also achieve a greater honey yield and higher profit margins. But even more importantly, the bees don't have to waste their energy to recreate new honeycombs each year. So modern hives definitely make bees happier. And increased profit margins make beekeepers happy. With these positive outcomes in mind, our plan is to grow the honey industry so that beekeeping can become a sustainable alternative to destructive logging in our irreplaceable ancient forests. Happy bees. Happy forests. And happy honey wine drinkers. Let's work together to increase the happiness!

In some places, we are already seeing the positive results of modernizing beekeeping in forested areas. Take, for example, Mama Christine, an entrepreneurial beekeeper in Kavwaya, Congo. Until recently, honey collectors in the lower Congo simply raided wild bee colonies in the forest, a practice that threatens forest bee populations. But Mama Christine knows that modern beekeeping increases honey yields and critically important bee populations. She recently harvested 75 liters of honey from her five hives, earning a single harvest profit that exceeds the amount most Congolese make in a year. And there are thousands of new beekeepers just like Mama Christine in the Congo. By fostering increased profits for beekeepers, we support local economies, provide alternatives to exploitative deforestation, and create increased biodiversity through pollination.

What other growing industry helps to bloom flowers and grow trees as a natural byproduct of business? While so much of what we consume negatively affects our environment, honey wine literally sustains it. Because bees will pollinate over two million flowers to make just one bottle of honey wine. And those two million flowers will germinate 20-40 million new seeds that contribute to healthy forests and fields upon fields of flowers.

All of this means that honey wine is deeply embedded in the cycle of nature. The ancients were on to something great when they made honey wine their drink of choice. It's now high time to return to honey wine. The bees and the earth demand it!

A Beeline for Urban Renewal

And it's not only forests that are benefiting from increased honey production. Increased attention to the crucial importance of bees has new hives popping up in some unexpected urban locations. In addition to cultivating an 1,100 square-foot vegetable garden on the South Lawn of the White House, Michelle Obama has also taken to amateur beekeeping in the heart of our nation's capital. And the move is much more than symbolic, as the bees pollinate her garden and provide up to 175 pounds of honey per year.

Best of all, the bees are entirely non-partisan, which means that neighboring politicians on both sides of the aisle have more bountiful gardens because of busy, presidential bees.

The private sector is equally invested in raising urban bee populations. The corporate offices of Google and

Intel each maintain hives on their roofs. And even the roof of New York City's Waldorf Astoria is home to a whopping 300,000 bees!

These bees produce about 800 pounds of honey a year, and believe it or not the Waldorf wants even more bees—their restaurants use about 1,000 pounds of honey a year. The Waldorf understands that young, environmentally conscious foodies appreciate locally sourced foods, and there's nothing more local than flower nectar from Central Park making it to your French toast in the Waldorf.

In San Francisco, a local organic market is also getting into rooftop beekeeping. Bi-Rite Market is located in the densely populated Mission District, but most residents are unaware that the bees are even there - that is, except for the locals who know where to find the best honey in town. Bi-Rite market is the first to admit that their honey is a bit pricier than the honey you buy at a supermarket, but their customers realize the value in supporting local businesses and their new neighbors, the bees. Honey tastes uniquely different in every locality because each location produces unique taste distinctions based on the flora around the hives. For San Francisco locals, the signature pleasures of Mission District honey is worth the higher cost.

Why You Should Keep It Local

But buying local honey is not only about the refined taste of neighborhood foodies. There are lots of reasons to go local, but perhaps the most valuable consequence

of buying local honey is to fight Colony Collapse Disorder. Increased demand for local honey raises local prices and encourages more people to go into beekeeping. This means that there are more bees and more hives dispersed over a wider area, which helps to tilt the odds in favor of bees threatened by CCD.

By buying honey locally, you also insure that your honey is produced in the most sustainable and healthy way possible. As it stands today, the United States consumes about 400 million pounds of honey a year, 52% of which is shipped in from mega-producers around the world. While the carbon footprint from shipping honey thousands of miles before consumption is cause enough to encourage buying local, there are also growing health concerns around the international flow of honey. A recent *Food Safety News* investigation reveals that foreign sourced honey from large-scale producers often has a presence of lead and illegal animal antibiotics. And this is when the honey actually comes from bees. Apparently, greed has driven international honey smugglers (yep, they exist!) to concoct "honey" made from artificial sweeteners.

There are very good reasons to protect the high quality of locally sourced American honey. And the same can be said for sustainable, coops that responsibly produce honey around the world. The important thing is to think small when you purchase honey, so avoid the mega-producers and seek out artisanal honey whenever it's humanly possible. Honey is so nutritionally beneficial that you owe it to yourself to consume the very best.

Moreover, by increasing pollination in the places your food actually comes from, you get a direct benefit to your nutrition. Researchers estimate that 40% of essential vitamins, minerals, and dietary lipids could be lost in areas where pollinators aren't present. So let's keep those pollinators employed in our local crops. And let's help encourage local beekeepers to produce all the honey and bees we need for a sustainable, healthy, and tasty future.

An Un-Industrial Revolution

Picture, if you will, the beauty of a grape wine vineyard as it sprawls over hill and dale for miles and miles. The beauty is uncontestable, but it sure does take up a lot of space. And what about all the mechanization required to run a vineyard compared to an apiary? Vineyards require irrigation systems, heavy machinery, fuel-burning tractors, climate controlling turbines, and often pesticides to control insects. And all of these things negatively effect our rivers, streams, and ground water.

In contrast, apiaries are not highly mechanized operations. Because running an apiary is an artisanal craft that involves working with nature, rather than against it. And while all the mechanization of a vineyard minimizes human labor, honey cultivation demands direct human interaction with hives. More human labor means jobs that stimulate local economies. Moreover, vineyards often negatively impact the environment by spreading fertilizer over large areas, controlling weeds with chemicals and roto-tillers, and putting a strain on our precious water resources.

The beauty of apiaries is that they thrive harmoniously in small spaces without negatively impacting the environment. In fact, honey is just a byproduct of bees making the world bountiful with wholesome foods and beautiful flowers.

Honey wine is without a doubt the most sustainable alcoholic beverage in history. What made it great in the past, makes it an even greater option for a sustainable future.

Now we just need to get our message out. So don't just drink honey wine! You'll also want to spread the good news about the role honey wine can play in giving us a more sustainable future.

Chapter V. A Beverage of Mythical Proportions

Myths and legends look at history from a different angle. Are they 100% true? Probably not. But in some ways, myths and legends contain more truth than can be held in any scholar's book. And honey wine is one of those uncontainable forces that only myth can begin to explain. The best way to experience honey wine is to drink it with reverence and knowledge. To help with the knowledge part, read below. As for the reverence? That will come naturally.

Honeymoon in Babylon

Did you know that the word "honeymoon" comes from the ancient tradition of giving the gift of honey wine to newlyweds? Well, that's what legend tells us, anyway. It's said that newly married couples in ancient Babylon were given gifts of golden honey wine on their wedding day. And as if this wasn't awesome enough, the newlyweds were directed to drink honey wine every night for a full

moon cycle to celebrate their vows—hence, the word "honeymoon." Pretty cool, huh?

A full month of honey wine? A great time for sure! But behind every ritual lies a purpose, and the purpose here was probably about making babies. You have to remember that elder family members arranged most ancient marriages, meaning that newlyweds had to get to "know" each other pretty quickly after the wedding. Drinking honey wine for a moon cycle would sort of smooth things over, if you know what we mean. But let's not be too practical about all of this. The ancients saw real power in honey wine, so let's indulge in the magic.

Honey Love

The Babylonians weren't the only ones to believe that honey is liquid love. Before Bacchus was known as the "God of Wine" the ancient Greeks called him "The Honey-Lord," which makes perfect sense given that honey wine likely predates grape wine.

The Honey-Lord was the god of ecstasy, ritual madness, and fertility. He carried a staff dripping with honey to represent the intoxicating effect of fermented honey and the sexual potency it was supposed to bequeath on imbibers.

The Honey-Lord apparently did a great job at sharing the aphrodisiac qualities of honey wine, because so many cultures think of the libation as erotically stimulating. In the Rig-Veda, a gathering of ancient Hindu Sanskrit hymns, honey wine is described as having the power to give wedded couples strong, healthy sons. And there are uncountable Old Norse tails in which honey wine is the means by which amorous gods convince unwilling partners to dally in love.

In medieval North Africa, the Moors gifted honey wine at weddings, believing that fermented honey is a love stimulant that produces bountiful families. The Greeks of course had honey wine drenched festivals that concluded in wild orgies. And a prominent Roman soldier serving under Julius Caesar writes very descriptively on how local Welsh honey wine gave him vigorous sexual powers while serving in the British Isles. But we may need to hear more from his alleged lovers to confirm this bit of boastful information.

While honey wine apparently has awesome powers for inspiring passion, you'll want to use moderation while tapping into this advantage. Take, for example, the plight of Hippocleides, an infamous Greek bachelor who lost his chance for love by enjoying too much honey wine.

As the story goes, Hippocleides was on the verge of marrying a beautiful (and rich) young girl before he drank liberal amounts of honey wine at a party hosted by his fiancée's father. Apparently, Hippocleides went frat-boy crazy on the dance floor, which included him standing on his head while kicking his legs furiously in the air.

The father of his fiancée was not impressed. So he said, "Oh son of Teisander, you have just danced away your marriage." Hippocleides blithely responded, "*οὐ φροντὶς Ἱπποκλείδῃ*," which translates roughly to "No worries for Hippocleides." And maybe he wasn't worried—at least not on that night. The next day, however, his bachelorhood was not in doubt.

The moral of the story? It could be said that a little honey wine inspires ardent romantic passion, while too much honey wine results in the opposite. You've been warned.

Before you go chalking up the aphrodisiac powers of honey wine as pure myth, consider this: honey wine is rich in B vitamins, nitric oxide, and amino acids that have been proven to support reproductive health. But while testing the link between myth and science, don't forget the ancient party boy, Hippocleides moderation is a vital ingredient for success.

Poetic Inspiration

Love and poetry have been tightly intertwined throughout history, which makes it no surprise that love inducing honey wine is also a traditional metaphor for divine, poetic inspiration. Listen up, aspiring poets. Because our greatest bards have long known that honey wine leads to the heights of poetic expression.

Long before Frances Meres referred to our most celebrated poet as "mellifluous & honey-tongued Shakespeare," honey wine was considered *the* prime source of poetry. In Norse mythology, anyone who drank the legendary *Mead of Suttungmjaðar* would become an eminent poet and scholar. Those who were lucky enough to partake in the *Mead of Suttungmjaðar* enjoyed a famous batch of honey wine with a complicated past.

Legend tells us that there was a long war between two factions of Norse Gods called the Æsir and the Vanir. After the war, the rival gods sealed a truce by spitting in a vat. From their intermingled saliva these gods created a man named Kvasir who could answer any question posed to him.

This legendary wise man travelled the world answering questions, but along the way he ran into some evil dwarves who murdered him and then mixed his blood into a batch of honey wine. This mixture resulted in the Mead of Poetry, believed to imbue the drinker with great wisdom.

To make a long story short, a giant named Suttungr was about to kill these evil dwarves, but was convinced to spare them in exchange for their magical honey wine. Suttungr then tried to hide the powerful potion away, but in short time Odin (the Norse god of wisdom, poetry, and magic) stole the golden elixir away by transforming himself into an eagle. Suttungr also took the shape of an eagle to pursue the thieving god, but he only managed to make Odin spill a portion of honey wine that has since been known as the "rhymester's share."

This small yet magical share of honey wine is responsible for inspiring our greatest poets. It's entertaining to imagine Dante, Chaucer, and Shakespeare getting their poetic genius by taking precious sips of divinely sourced honey wine. And while you might not be lucky enough to find the legendary "rhymester's share," you can indulge in the same pleasure that initiated thousands of years of myth and legend. All you need to do is fit the right bottle of honey wine to the right occasion - the poetry will surely happen.

Chapter VI. "Must" Knows about Fermentation

It's so simple. Take water, mix in honey, add optional herbs, hops, spices, and then...wait. The resulting concoction is called the "must." Once you have the must, all you have to do is wait for naturally occurring yeasts in the air to mix with your creation, and *voila*! You've got honey wine. This is how the ancients first made honey wine, and what worked for them, will also work for you. So what are you waiting for? Okay, you're probably waiting for a little more information, so here goes...

Flowers Live in the Bouquet of Honey

Two core ingredients influence the taste and bouquet of traditional honey wine: honey and yeast. Much like grape appellations distinguish the character of grape wines, the floral origins of honey and the type of yeast used will determine the distinct taste of your own honey wine creations.

One of the purest joys of honey wine is that honey absorbs the fragrance of blossoming flowers. So if your wine is based in sage honey, hints of sage will dance on your palate when you first taste your wine. Or if you choose to use jasmine honey, you'll be taken on an olfactory journey to the time you first walked by a blooming jasmine bush. In this way, honey wine comes with a distinct memory—a memory of life in bloom.

A wide range of floral pleasures awaits the adventurous honey wine maker, including: acacia, buckwheat, eucalyptus, clover, mesquite, orange-blossom, sage, and even pepperwood. If bees are attracted to a flower, that flower can become an integral part of your wine.

Be sure to do your research while experimenting with honey types. For example, every culture favors a certain type of honey over others, which probably has as much to do with cultural values as it does with floral ubiquity. In Poland honey wine is a staple drink, and the Poles love using dark buckwheat honey with a robust, stout character. Buckwheat is readily available for bees in the area, making the local honey wine a true reflection of the region it hails from. This means that honey wine has a *terroir* (or sense of place) in just the same way as grape wine does.

How much honey should you use for your must? Well, that depends on how sweet you like your honey wine. But keep in mind that the more honey you use, the stronger the alcohol content in your final product. This is because more honey means more food for the yeast (this is true up to the point when the alcohol becomes so strong that it kills off the yeast).

The recommended range for crafting successful honey wine is anywhere from 2½ to 5 pounds of honey per each gallon of water. Unless of course you're interested in making Polish *Dwójniak*. This traditional beverage sports a strong alcohol content resulting from using equal parts honey and water. The Poles drink more honey wine than most other cultures—maybe the secret is in the *Dwójniak*. We'll leave that for you to investigate.

Holy Yeasties!

We should all pause a moment to worship the all holy yeasts. Without them, there'd be no wine or beer of any sort. Yes, you heard that right. As you try to recover from the thought of life without yeast, rest assured that there are more yeast cells in the world than can be humanly comprehended. The future is secure.

The sole job of the yeast is to digest sugars. Wouldn't it be nice if you too could find a job that just asked you to eat? Actually, you could secure such a job if the byproduct of your eating produced alcohol and carbon dioxide—at least, that's what yeast do. And we are all greatly beholden to the digestive habits of these busy little fungi. And what "fun guys" they are—sorry, it's hard to pass on good yeast humor.

As we mentioned earlier, yeast occur naturally in our environment, so fermentation can happen without any human assistance. But with the invention of select strains of yeast in the late 18th century, pitching yeasts into must has become a common practice. Over the years, hundreds of yeast strains have been distributed under numerous brand names. The way that Champagne yeasts interact with honey have given them prominence in honey wine production, but there are some yeast strains created specifically for fermenting honey wine. Do yourself a favor and explore the possibilities.

But not so fast. Ethiopians have maintained the ancient practice of producing honey wines at home with naturally occurring yeasts. This means that almost every family has an *ensera* (a clay keg) tucked away in a dark corner of the house. A wide range of the population enjoys these homemade honey wines—even Muslims in Ethiopia consume the must before the yeast kicks in and starts producing alcohol. Recall that this non-alcoholic beverage is called *berz*. But to be sure, inhabitants of other faiths in Ethiopia hold out while yeast produce a welcome alcoholic kick.

Good Chemistry Means Good Wine

For the chemists out there who still know their molar weights, here is the reaction that occurs in honey wine fermentation (the reactions within yeast cells are quite complex, so this is the easy version):

$$C_6H_{12}O_{12} \rightarrow 2(CH_3CH_2O_2) + 2(CO_2) + Energy$$

Sugar   Alcohol   Carbon dioxide

The sugar is digested and converted to alcohol and the byproducts are carbon dioxide and heat generation. There are also a host of other issues specific to honey wine fermentation. For example, honey is low in naturally occurring yeast nutrients (what yeast eat), so you might have to add additional nutrients to keep the yeast on a balanced diet that keeps them fit for fermentation duty.

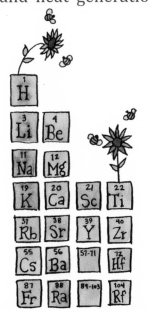

Another issue to look out for is acidity. Honey water can get acidic very quickly, which dramatically inhibits fermentation levels. Since fermentation is the key, you'll need to closely monitor acid levels throughout the process.

And finally, naturally occurring proteins in honey can cause cloudiness in homemade honey wines. If you want that brilliant, gemlike hue of a superior glass of honey wine, you'll want to boil the honey/water mixture prior to fermentation so you can skim the proteins off the top. But take heed, boiling will take away some of the fragrant properties of the honey. Or instead of boiling you can always rent a filter from your local brewery supply store. You've got some decisions to make.

Follow the Yellow Brick Road

Ancient honey wine was probably more yellow than the more golden tones we've become accustomed to in the modern era. This is because the ancients used traditional beehives and did not extract the honey from the honeycomb prior to fermentation, as is the practice today. By fermenting the honey comb-and-all, the overall product had a much higher pollen content. If you have the opportunity to drink *t'ej* made in Ethiopia, you'll quickly appreciate what a high pollen count does to the color and taste of honey wine—it's as if you're drinking nectar straight from the flower.

There are honey wine aficionados that appreciate traditional yellow tones, and there are those that set a high price on golden clarity. In the end, this is a personal preference. But in terms of modern production, the extent to which honey wine reflects golden hues is dependent on the level at which the wine is filtered, the ratio of honey used proportionate to water, and the duration of fermentation.

Got Gesho?

Ah, the elusive pleasures of gesho. But the question is this: to gesho or not to gesho?
To answer this question you must consider how (and if) you want to balance the natural sweetness of unadulterated honey wine. Gesho comes from the stalks of a buckthorn bush (*Rhamnus prinoides*), and it works in honey wine much the same way that hops

do in beer. Gesho offers a way to retain traditional honey wine techniques while also providing a sophisticated balancing effect to the sweetness of honey.

There are many ways to get gesho into your mix: some boil it first, others smoke it prior to fermentation (not  in cigarette papers, people). But most Ethiopians just toss handfuls of gesho right into the *ensera*. In Ethiopia, most see gesho as a catalyst for fermentation, and while modern chemists scoff at this belief, it could be that the ancient tradition got it right. Because gesho naturally boosts the nutrients yeast require to ferment honey efficiently. Anyway, a nation of 90 million devoted honey wine drinkers can't be all wrong, right?

Ethiopians are so wild about gesho they even dedicated a stamp to the bitter, little shrub. And you'll have trust us: the plant has a *much* more appealing look than the stamp would suggest.

Do Try This at Home

While this has been a fast and furious introduction to fermenting honey wine, there are a number of great websites and books devoted entirely to making homemade honey wine—part of the pleasure is learning, and there are some great resources available. Thanks to President Jimmy Carter, making your own honey wine has been legal since 1978. And hey, nobody will ask you to verify your age while you're buying honey and yeast (you're making a French loaf, right?). Best of all, the whole process is fool proof. After all, in what other craft can you drink all of your mistakes?

As a final note, avoid bathing for at least a week if you're going to make your batch in the bathtub. It's a matter of courtesy, people.

For now, just make a beeline to your local bookstore for these three excellent books:

- *Making Mead (Honey Wine)* by Roger Morse
- *The Compleat Meadmaker* by Ken Schramm
- *Mad about Mead!* by Pamela Spence

Chapter VII. The Rebirth of Honey Wine

As you now know, honey wine is deeply imbedded in our global history, mythologies, and cultures. And yet all that came before is mere prologue to the vibrant rebirth honey wine is enjoying in modern culture. As Michael Sanders puts it in a recent article in *The New York Times*, honey wine is "so old, it's new."

The "so old, it's new" phenomenon has been sweeping through our culture in other forms, as well. For example, heightened awareness about how food distribution impacts the environment has inspired foodies to seek out locally sourced foods whenever possible. This awareness has led to farmers markets springing up in almost every local community. And lest hip, young foodies think they invented organic farmers markets,  we'll have to remind them that these open marketplaces are as old as, well, honey wine. In fact, maybe we've finally found a cultural phenomenon that actually predates honey wine.

The real point is this: people want to enjoy the finer things of life in a socially responsible way, and sometimes the historic past can teach us how to do this. Farmer's markets are one example of an old world tradition returning as a hip, responsible lifestyle. But farmers markets did need a bit of a makeover to make this happen (you probably couldn't get truffle goat cheese at ye' olde farmers market).

If you've been following our story, you know that every culture reinvents honey wine to suit the respective needs, desires, and tastes of its people. From honey wines that occurred naturally in the nooks of baobab trees, to honey wines infused with bacon, the story of honey wine is one of evolution and transcendence.

But there were dark times when it took monks to keep the tradition alive. And there were times of scarcity when the common man could not find honey wine at all. But in the end, we're very lucky that our Ethiopian and Polish friends took care of a honey wine tradition that we can all learn from today. And hey, after 200,000 years of glorious honey wine tradition, a 300-year decline in consumption is equivalent to just one bad financial quarter!

So today we proudly proclaim an end to The Great Honey Wine Recession! Because we now have polished, modern styles of honey wine for a new age of imbibers. We can now enjoy dry-hopped varieties that rival any aridly refined Sauvignon Blanc, effervescent honey wines that provide a celebratory alternative to champagne, and to-die-for dessert varieties that bring new meaning to after dinner indulgence.

Even the liquor industry sees a future in the blissful relationship between honey and alcohol. The great American distillers at Jack Daniel's recently launched a whiskey called "Tennessee Honey," which is an "undeniably smooth" liquor that boasts "a honeysuckle nose and tasting notes of praline, caramel, butter, and, of course, wild honey." White House chefs are even getting in on the honey craze, having concocted a home brew called "White House Honey Ale" for President Obama. Our inside sources describe the home brew as a "lovely auburn brown" ale with floral aromas.

Now that honey wine and honey-based libations are all the rage, what's left to do? Well, friends, that is up to you. We can only bring you the honey wine story. It's now up to *you* to write the next chapter. So call your friends and neighbors! And invite them over to enjoy the oldest, new drink on the scene. It's good for our bees! It's good for our planet! And it's simply the right time to rewrite the story of honey wine.

With this in mind, we ask you to take over the story of honey wine. Because only you can drive the rebirth of the most noble beverage in history. Along the way, send us your pictures.

Tell us your honey wine stories. Where did you first try honey wine? What do you serve honey wine with?

Where's your favorite place to drink honey wine? Is it really an aphrodisiac?

Now is your chance to create history. Bring it back and make it epic!

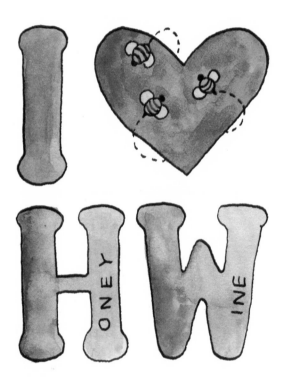

Acknowledgements

This book was born from the collaboration of six talented professionals living in California, Colorado, Pennsylvania and Porto, Portugal.

Randy Johnson – Script
randyjohnson.johnson@gmail.com

Lindsey Bugbee – Illustrations
lindsey@thepostmansknock.com

Suzanne Musikantow – Podcast narration
suzmusikantow@comcast.net

Diogo Lando – Cover design
mail@diogolando.com

Jane Shaffer – Layout and book design
jshaffer@missionoss.com

Harry Kloman – Proofreading and editing
kloman@pitt.edu

How to Order Honey Wine in Any Land

Language	"Honey Wine"	Country
Aari	s'ajji	Ethiopia
Afar	malb, gohoyu (honey beer)	Ethiopia
Alaaba	daat'a	Ethiopia
Amharic	t'ej, berz (non-alcohol)	Ethiopia
Anfillo	bita	Ethiopia
Anuak	ogool, ocatha (honey beer)	Ethiopia
Arabic	nabidh	Middle East & North Africa
Arbore	d'aadi	Ethiopia
Argobba	t'ej	Ethiopia
Awngi	mishi	Ethiopia
Baiso	t'ejji	Ethiopia
Baka	njambu	Cameroon
Bamana (Mande group)	diji, dikolen	Mali
Bambassi	bit'	Ethiopia
Banda-Banda	duma	Central African Republic
Barbaig (d. Datooga)	gesuda	Tanzania
Basketo	t'ej	Ethiopia
Bedawi	adarha	Sudan
Bemba	mbote/imbote	Zambia
Bench	es	Ethiopia
Berta	baas'a	Ethiopia
Bilin	mes/miys, mid	Eritrea
Birale (nearly extinct)	koronko	Ethiopia
Bobo	básè	Burkina Faso
Bodi	gema, gemade boorini	Ethiopia
Bomu	so	Mali
Boni	bo'or	Tanzania
Boro	bito	Ethiopia
Breton	chouchen	France
Bulgarian	medovina	Bulgaria
Burji	boka/booka	Ethiopia
Bussa	t'ayye	Ethiopia
Chaha	dagye, dege	Ethiopia
Chai	gimáy, t'acc	Ethiopia
Chara	eesa	Ethiopia

Cheyenne	hahnomâhep - ano'êhaseo'o tseve'keeno'e	U.S.A.
Chinese (Mandarin, Cantonese)	mì jiû, mat zau	China, Taiwan
Czech	medovina	Czech Republic
Daasanach	thaaniti, t'ej	Ethiopia
Dahalo	mola	Kenya
Danish	mjød	Denmark
Dime	tajj	Ethiopia
Dinka	dhum, dhumo	Sudan
Dirasha	t'ajjet tanket	Ethiopia
Dizi	t'ej	Ethiopia
Dogon	bédji	Mali
Dorze	t'ej	Ethiopia
Dutch	mede	Netherlands
English	mead, meodu (historical)	Britain & other countries
Estonian	mõdu	Estonia
Falashan	miz	Ethiopia
Finnish	sima	Finland
Flemish	mede	Belgium
French	hydromel	France & other countries
Gafat (extinct)	s'aj	Ethiopia
Galila	s'ajji	Ethiopia
Gamo-Gofa-Dawro	t'ej, 'ees (Gamo)	Ethiopia
Gawwada	t'ayye	Ethiopia
Ge'ez (liturgical)	s'ajj, mes/miys	Ethiopia
Gedeo	boka/booka	Ethiopia
German	met, medu (historical)	Germany
Gogot/Dobi	dag'a, t'ej	Ethiopia
Greek	ydromeli	Greece
Gula	duma	Central African Republic
Gumuz	ke'e'-ka'tsha	Ethiopia
Gurage	t'ej	Ethiopia
Hadiyya	dik'aasa	Ethiopia
Hamer-Banna	zia (Hamer), ant'si (Banna)	Ethiopia
Harari	t'ajji, gohoy (honey beer)	Ethiopia
Hebrew	temad, yeyin dvash	Israel
Hozo	bit'	Ethiopia
Hungarian	mézbor	Hungary
Icelandic	mjöõur	Iceland
Igbo	mmanya anyu	Nigeria
Indonesian	padang rumput	Indonesia

Inor	dag'a, t'ej	Ethiopia
Italian	idromele	Italy
Japanese	hachimitsu sake	Japan
Kadaru (Kafir)	i-qilika	Sudan
Kafa	bito	Ethiopia
Kambaata	daat'a	Ethiopia
Kaonde	mbote/imbote	Zambia
Karo	ala, sia	Ethiopia
Kikamba, Kikuyu, Imenti	uki/uuki	Kenya
Kirundi	ubuki	Burundi
Kistane/Soddo	t'ej	Ethiopia
Komo	biti	Ethiopia
Komso	taadita, tajjeeta	Ethiopia
Koorete	t'eje, shida dana, sh'ádzhe, caje	Ethiopia
Korean	kkul sul	Korea
Kunfal	mishi	Ethiopia
Kwama	biti	Ethiopia
Kwegu	ítire	Ethiopia
Kxoe	dini-caca	Namibia
Lamba	mbote/imbote	Zambia
Libido	dik'aasa (non-alcoholic)	Ethiopia
Lithuanian	midus	Lithuania
Luchazi	bingundo	Angola
Lunda	kosolo/kasolu	Zambia
Luvale	ndoka	Zambia
Maa (Maasai Maa)	enaisho olotorok	Tanzania, Kenya
Maale	dago	Ethiopia
Majang	ogool	Ethiopia
Mamara Senoufo	se cunahara	Mali
Mande group	liji/diji	Benin, Burkina Faso, Mali & Nigeria
Mayan	balche, pitarilla	Mexico & other countries
Mbunda	migundo	Angola, Zambia
Me'en	gima, boké	Ethiopia
Melo	'ess, 'eesa	Ethiopia
Mesqan	dag'a, t'ej	Ethiopia
Moru	duma	Sudan
Muher	dagye, dege	Ethiopia
Mursi	gimma	Ethiopia

Nandi	kipketinik	Democratic Republic of Congo
Ndebele	mbote/imbote	Zambia
Ndogo	pili	Sudan
Nguni group	amambawu	South Africa, Swaziland, Zimbabwe
Nkoya	mbote/imbote	Zambia
Norwegian	mjød	Norway
Nuer	koang twaar	Ethiopia
Nyamwezi	wanzuki	Tanzania
Nyangatom	a-tede	Ethiopia
Nyanja	kachasu	Malawi
Opuuo	biti	Ethiopia
Oromo	daad'ii	Ethiopia
Persian	mey	Iran
Polish	miòd	Poland
Portuguese	hidromel	Portugal, Brazil, & other countries
Pulaar Fulfulde	bese/besu, kokoni	Mali
Qabena	tajjita	Ethiopia
Qimant	miz	Ethiopia
Russian	medovukha	Russia
Rwanda	funguro	Rwanda
Saho	mees, bathce, malah (honey beer)	Ethiopia
Sango	duma	Central African Republic
Sanskrit	madhu	India
Serbo-Croatian	medovina	Serbia & Crotia
Seze	bit'	Ethiopia
Shabo	oo	Ethiopia
Shekkacho	bito	Ethiopia
Sheko	taka	Ethiopia
Sidama	malawo/malabo, t'ajje	Ethiopia
Silt'e	tajji	Ethiopia
Slovak	medovina	Slovakia
Slovenian	medica	Slovenia
Somali	khamri malabeed	Ethiopia
Songo	quingundo	Democratic Republic of Congo

Spanish	aguamiel	Spain & other countries
Swahili	mvinyo/pombe, ya asali	East African
Swedish	mjöd	Sweden
Tagalog	idromel, agwamyel	Philippines
Tigrinya	mes/miys	Ethiopia & Eritrea
Tirma	gimáy, t'acc	Ethiopia
Tsamai	xoronko	Ethiopia
Tsonga	vhinya/wayeni/ya vulombe	South Africa, others
Tswana	khadi	Botswana, others
Turkana	epurot a aowu/aoo	Ethiopia
Uduk	t'ej, asum ayin	Ethiopia
Ukranian	med	Ukrain
Vietnamese	mâtruou	Vietnam
Welsh	meddeglyn or myddyglyn	Britain
Wolane	t'ajay	Ethiopia
Wolayta	'essa	Ethiopia
Wolof	sibah/sibarrh/sibax	Senegal
Xamtanga	miz	Ethiopia
Xhosa	iQhilika	Botswana, Lesotho, South Africa
Yemsa	éésa	Ethiopia
Zande, Lingala	duma/dumu	Democratic Republic of Congo
Zergulla	c'ajj	Ethiopia
Zigula	wischa	Tanzania
Zulu	uhlobo, lotshwala, iwayini loju	South Africa
Zway	sexär, t'eje	Ethiopia

Source

http://www.pitt.edu/~kloman/tej.html
http://www.solorb.com/mead/